3D OBJECTS

Discovering Cones

Nancy Furstinger
and John Willis

MEDIA ENHANCED BOOKS
AV2 BY WEIGL
ADDED VALUE • AUDIO VISUAL
www.av2books.com

AV^2 provides enriched content that supplements and complements this book. Weigl's AV^2 books strive to create inspired learning and engage young minds in a total learning experience.

Your AV^2 Media Enhanced books come alive with...

Audio
Listen to sections of the book read aloud.

Key Words
Study vocabulary, and complete a matching word activity.

Video
Watch informative video clips.

Quizzes
Test your knowledge.

Embedded Weblinks
Gain additional information for research.

Slide Show
View images and captions, and prepare a presentation.

Try This!
Complete activities and hands-on experiments.

... and much, much more!

MEDIA ENHANCED BOOKS AV^2 BY WEIGL™ ADDED VALUE • AUDIO VISUAL

Go to www.av2books.com, and enter this book's unique code.

BOOK CODE

X386664

AV^2 by Weigl brings you media enhanced books that support active learning.

Published by AV^2 by Weigl
350 5th Avenue, 59th Floor
New York, NY 10118
www.av2books.com

Library of Congress Cataloging-in-Publication Data

Names: Furstinger, Nancy, author. | Willis, John, 1989-, author.
Title: Discovering cones / Nancy Furstinger and John Willis.
Description: New York, NY : AV2 by Weigl, [2016] | Series: 3D objects | Includes bibliographical references and index.
Identifiers: LCCN 2016005491 (print) | LCCN 2016012624 (ebook) | ISBN 9781489649713 (hard cover : alk. paper) | ISBN 9781489649720 (soft cover : alk. paper) | ISBN 9781489649737 (Multi-user ebk.)
Subjects: LCSH: Cone--Juvenile literature. | Geometry, Solid--Juvenile literature.
Classification: LCC QA491 .F865 2016 (print) | LCC QA491 (ebook) | DDC 516.156--dc23
LC record available at https://lccn.loc.gov/2016005491

Printed in the United States of America in Brainerd, Minnesota
1 2 3 4 5 6 7 8 9 0 20 19 18 17 16

082016
210716

Project Coordinator: John Willis Art Director: Terry Paulhus

Every reasonable effort has been made to trace ownership and to obtain permission to reprint copyright material. The publishers would be pleased to have any errors or omissions brought to their attention so that they may be corrected in subsequent printings.

Weigl acknowledges Getty Images, Alamy, and iStock as its primary image suppliers for this title.

CONTENTS

WRITING WITH ICING

You baked a delicious cake for your friend's birthday. Now you need to decorate it. You fill up an icing tube with pink icing. You slowly squeeze the icing out of the pointy tip and write your friend's name. Now your cake is ready for the birthday party. Do not forget to pass out the party hats so everyone can celebrate.

Did you notice how the shape of the icing tube tip matches the shape of the party hats? Both of these shapes are **cones**.

Can you think of any other things at a party that might be shaped like a cone?

WHAT DOES A CONE LOOK LIKE?

Cones are all around us. Cones are shapes that have three **dimensions**. They are not flat. Shapes that are flat, such as a circle, have only two dimensions, length and width. These flat shapes are also called plane shapes or 2D shapes.

Shapes such as cones that have three dimensions are called **3D** shapes. We can measure all three dimensions of a cone, its length, width, and height. 3D shapes are also called solid shapes.

Cone-shaped megaphones help to make people's voices louder.

Witches' hats are cone-shaped. They are pointy at the top and wide at the bottom.

HOW DO WE KNOW A SHAPE IS A CONE?

If a cone is cut into short sections, only the one at the top is still a cone. It is the only section that still has a point.

A cone has a flat, round bottom called a **base**. If you trace around a cone's base, you draw a circle. The flat circle forms one **face** of the cone. A face is a two-dimensional flat **surface**.

Each cone has a curved surface as well. The cone's curved surface wraps around the circle. This curving side forms an **edge** where it comes together with the circular base. The curved surface also forms a corner that is shaped like a point. This corner is called a **vertex**.

PARTS OF A CONE

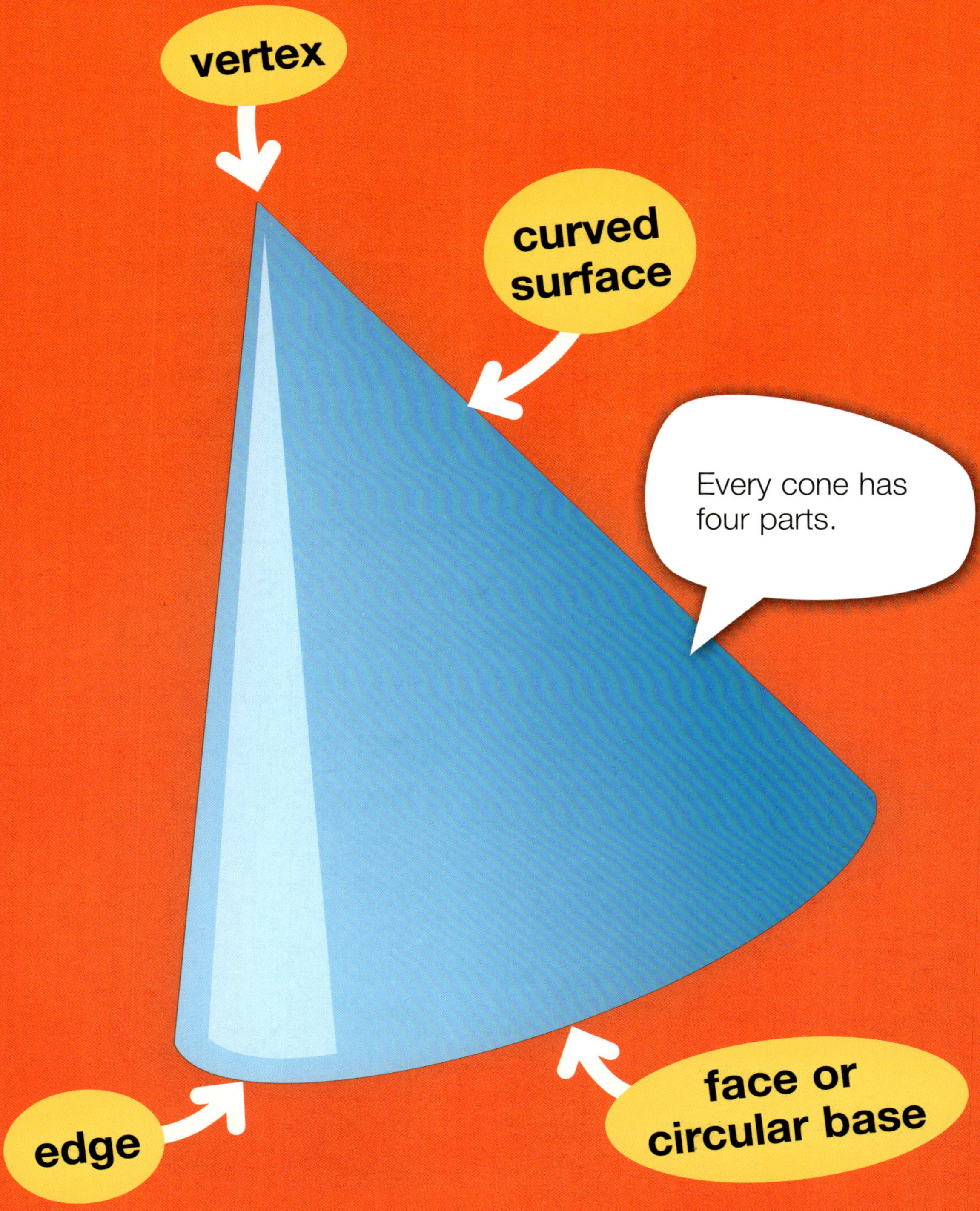

CONES AT WORK

Once you know what a cone looks like, you can easily spot this 3D shape. You will start to see cones everywhere.

If there is a gigantic pothole in the street, bright orange-and-white-striped traffic cones will mark the spot. When people see these cones, they will know to drive carefully.

The earliest traffic cones were made of concrete. Today, plastic cones bounce back if they are run over. Traffic cones come in other colors, but orange is the most popular.

The shape of traffic cones makes them easy to stack.

CONES AT PLAY

Your class is putting on a play. You volunteer to help build the scenery. Your castle rises tall and straight. Your friend tells you to add a tower. You crown the tower with a cone. Now you have built a splendid castle.

The princess in the play wears a hat in the shape of a cone. This cone-shaped headdress became popular with European women in the Middle Ages. A see-through veil floated down the back. Some headdresses stood 3 feet (1 meter) high. They were so tall that women had problems walking through doorways.

In the Middle Ages, stiff cloth or wire mesh formed the frames of these conical hats. They were covered with light fabric, such as silk.

ICE CREAM CONES

The most well-known cone holds scoops of ice cream. You can choose a sugar cone, a wafer cone, or a waffle cone. Fancy cones are dipped in chocolate. Then, they are rolled in candy sprinkles or nuts. Machines in factories can make 150,000 cones every day. Imagine how much ice cream would be needed to fill that many cones.

You might see ice cream cones stored in tall stacks in an ice cream shop.

The first ice cream cone was invented in New York City in 1896. Another version of this tasty ice cream holder appeared at the 1904 Saint Louis World's Fair. When an ice cream seller ran out of dishes, a man selling waffle pastry had an idea. He rolled a waffle into a cone shape, creating the waffle cone.

Cones were not the first edible ice cream container. In the late 1800s, ice cream was sometimes sold in edible biscuit bowls with flat bottoms.

LIVING IN A CONE

Some people lived in cone-shaped tents. Native Americans who roamed the Great Plains until the 1800s brought along portable homes called tepees. Tepees offered Native Americans a snug and weather-tight home.

Ten to twenty poles gave the tepee its cone-shaped structure. Then, it was covered with buffalo or elk hides. There was an opening at the top, and smoke flaps at the sides. These allowed people inside the tepee to cook over an open fire and stay warm.

The cone-shaped tents were easy to take apart. The bundle of hides and poles was easy to drag. At first, the Native Americans used dogs to help move their homes from place to place. Later, when horses arrived on the Plains, Native Americans switched to horsepower. Since horses were stronger, they could drag longer poles. Tepees rose higher, up to 20 feet (6 m) tall, or about the height of five children.

Modern-day tepees are covered with cloth. Now, they last longer and are lighter. Tepees are the perfect shelter for camping.

Today, tepees come in all different sizes.

CONES IN ART

The artist Dennis Oppenheim created five gigantic traffic cones. He displayed them in Seattle's Olympic Sculpture Park. He named these giant pieces of art *Safety Cones*. The bright orange **fiberglass** cones each stand 18 feet (5.5 m) high. That is as tall as a giraffe.

Oppenheim's *Safety Cones* were also displayed in Italy, at Scolacium Archaeological Park.

CATCHING WIND IN A CONE

What type of cone shows you which direction and how fast the wind is blowing? It is a windsock, which got its name because it looks like a giant sock. The windsock is attached to the top of a pole, like a flag. When wind fills the windsock, it takes on the shape of a cone. The windsock droops if the wind is low. The windsock flies **parallel** to the ground if the wind is high.

Windsocks soar with the speed of wind at airports and alongside windy spots on highways. People also decorate their yards with bright windsocks.

CONES IN NATURE

You can find cone shapes in nature. Some colorful cone-shaped flowers rise on stalks. Many pine trees are shaped like cones. Their woody pinecones are named for their shape. They produce seeds from which new pine trees grow.

Most volcanoes form cone-shaped hills when they erupt. Two types of volcano cones are common. Cinder cones form when hot molten rock called lava is blown out of the volcano's vent, or opening. The tiny bits of lava look like cinders. Composite cones form after dramatic explosions. They are made up of layers of ash, lava, and broken rock.

Search for cone shapes wherever you go. You will be amazed how many of these 3D shapes you can discover in your house or out and about.

CONES QUIZ

1. What is the corner of a cone called?

2. When was the first ice cream cone invented?

3. What were the frames of conical hats made of during the Middle Ages?

4. What is another name for plane shapes?

5 Where is Mauna Loa located?

6 How do windsocks fly when the wind is high?

7 What is the most popular traffic cone color?

8 What is the flat bottom of a cone called?

Answers:
1. The vertex 2. In 1896 3. Stiff cloth or wire mesh 4. 2D shapes
5. In Hawai'i 6. Parallel to the ground 7. Orange 8. The base

ACTIVITY:
CREATE A CLOWN HAT

This cone-shaped hat is fun and easy to make. You can decorate your hat any way you want to.

Materials

- colored paper
- compass
- pencil
- scissors
- stapler
- glue
- stickers
- pompom

Directions

1. Use a compass to draw a half circle on paper. The half circle should be about 20 inches (50 cm) across.
2. Cut out the half circle.
3. Roll the shape into a cone.
4. Staple the cone at the base of the seam. Try the hat on and adjust if necessary. Then, glue the seam shut. Remove the staple when the glue is dry.
5. Decorate your clown hat with stickers. Top it with a pompom.

KEY WORDS

3D: a shape with length, width, and height

base: one of the flat surfaces of a 3D shape

cones: 3D shapes with circular bases that slope up to a point

dimensions: the length, width, or height of an object

edge: the line where a surface begins or ends

face: a flat surface on a 3D shape

fiberglass: a strong plastic material that contains glass fibers

parallel: lines that are always the same distance apart

surface: the flat or curved border of a 3D shape

vertex: the point where the edges of a 3D shape meet

INDEX

Log on to www.av2books.com

AV² by Weigl brings you media enhanced books that support active learning. Go to www.av2books.com, and enter the special code found on page 2 of this book. You will gain access to enriched and enhanced content that supplements and complements this book. Content includes video, audio, weblinks, quizzes, a slide show, and activities.

AV² Online Navigation

Audio
Listen to sections of the book read aloud.

Book Pages
AV² pages directly correspond to pages in the book.

Video
Watch informative video clips.

Embedded Weblinks
Gain additional information for research.

Key Words
Study vocabulary, and complete a matching word activity.

Try This!
Complete activities and hands-on experiments.

Quizzes
Test your knowledge.

Slide Show
View images and captions, and prepare a presentation.

AV² was built to bridge the gap between print and digital. We encourage you to tell us what you like and what you want to see in the future.

Sign up to be an AV² Ambassador at www.av2books.com/ambassador.

Due to the dynamic nature of the Internet, some of the URLs and activities provided as part of AV² by Weigl may have changed or ceased to exist. AV² by Weigl accepts no responsibility for any such changes. All media enhanced books are regularly monitored to update addresses and sites in a timely manner. Contact AV² by Weigl at 1-866-649-3445 or av2books@weigl.com with any questions, comments, or feedback.